An Elephant's Trunk

Leroy Taylor

An elephant has a very long trunk.

2

An elephant uses its trunk to smell.

An elephant uses its trunk to dig.

4

An elephant uses its trunk to eat.

5

An elephant uses its trunk to drink.

An elephant uses its trunk to wash.

7

An elephant uses its trunk to hug.

8